MW01644861

mindful contours

Copyright © 2024 Celina Caesar-Chavannes
All rights reserved.

This Experience Belongs to:

Transcend. Transform. Thrive.

Accept

There is no good.
There is no bad.
There just is.

If we trust that the universe always unfolds as it should, and that it always unfolds in our favour, then everything that happens should be accepted.

Learn the lesson from the experience with grace, gratitude, and acceptance.

Be. Breathe.

There is no need to panic,
stress, or worry.

Be still in the present moment.

Breathe.

In - 2, 3, 4
Hold - 2, 3, 4
and
Out - 2, 3, 4
Hold - 2, 3, 4

Repeat

Calm

Remain still and let all energy pass freely through you.

Accept the thoughts that come and go, and remain calm in the moment.

Anything that is disrupting this peace is too expensive. Do not pay any attention (or price) for it.

Don’t Doubt

Trust in the intelligence of the universe that is within, and all around, you.

When doubt creeps in, remember that you have all the tools within you to accomplish any task.

Energy

The energy you are,
is the energy you attract.

If negative energy emerges
in your day, accept it
+
Ask the universe to
transform it into something
amazing
+
Release it to the world.
=
Let nothing dim your light.

Flow. Frequency.

The higher the frequency of
your vibrations,
the brighter the light that
glows in, and from, you.

Remove everything
(internally and externally)
that blocks your high
frequency vibrations and
your natural flow.

Increase the flow of your
glow.

Gratitude

If you perform every act in service of others, ego cannot disrupt the entelechy of you.

Let every act, every situation, every moment, be experienced in gratitude and service to the whole.

Be wholē.

Heaven

You are what you think you are.
You are what you think you are not.

Both are correct.

Choose wisely.

Choose peace, love, joy, and ease.

Choose heaven.

Imagination

Your imagination is heaven.

A place where you can create
the world of your dreams.

A place of peace, joy, and
bliss.

Go ahead. Create it.
Feel all the feels.
Live the reality.

Joy

You cannot explain joy.

Sometimes you have this feeling that reaches beyond happiness into another dimension.

You have no reason for it. You have no explanation for it.

It is just joy.

Know

Know that you are enough.

Trust your gut and know
that your intuition is
correct.

Don’t simply believe in
yourself.
Know yourself so well that
you do not doubt.

When everything else fails,
know that you know.

Love

Love does not fight,
struggle, hurt, break,
cause pain, or induce
harm.

Love is easy.

If it isn't easy,
it isn't love.

Magic and Miracles

Magic is real.

Miracles are real.

Make them happen.

Extend your dreams beyond the
stars and into the heavens.
Into the love that is deep
within you.
That is where the magic and
miracles happen.

You are that power(full).

Namasté

I honour the divinity in you, which is also the divinity in me.

We are one.

Open

When you are rigid,
and following your
“planned life”
too closely,
you limit your options.

Open yourself up to the
infinite possibilities of the
universe.

Prayer

What is the difference between prayer and meditation?

Prayer is how you talk to the Creator.

Meditation is how you listen.

Quiet

You have nothing to prove.

You have nothing to defend.

You have nothing to explain.

It is ok to let them figure it
out on their own.

Be Still.
Be Quiet.

Re-member

Remembering is a journey toward reconnecting with your true essence and recognizing that you are an integral part of the universe.

It's about rediscovering the interconnectedness of all things and awakening to the reality that our individual consciousness is an important part of universal consciousness.

Synchronicities

Synchronicities are the little signs and coincidences that the universe sends to show you that you are on the right path.

Trust the process.
Follow the signs.

Do not worry about not getting things right or missing out.

You are in the right place.
This is the right time.

Time

There is no time.

Love the present.

Unity

It is not about you.
It is not about them.
It has always been
about us.

When we decide to stop
judging everything and
everyone, the last
judgement has occurred.

This is Atonement.

The *Moment* we recognize
that we are *At One*.

Vibration

When you understand and harness the power of your own vibrations, you hold the power to change your life.

‘Good vibes only’ is not just a slogan, it is a way of Being that releases and attracts what you are to the world.

Be the good vibes the world needs.

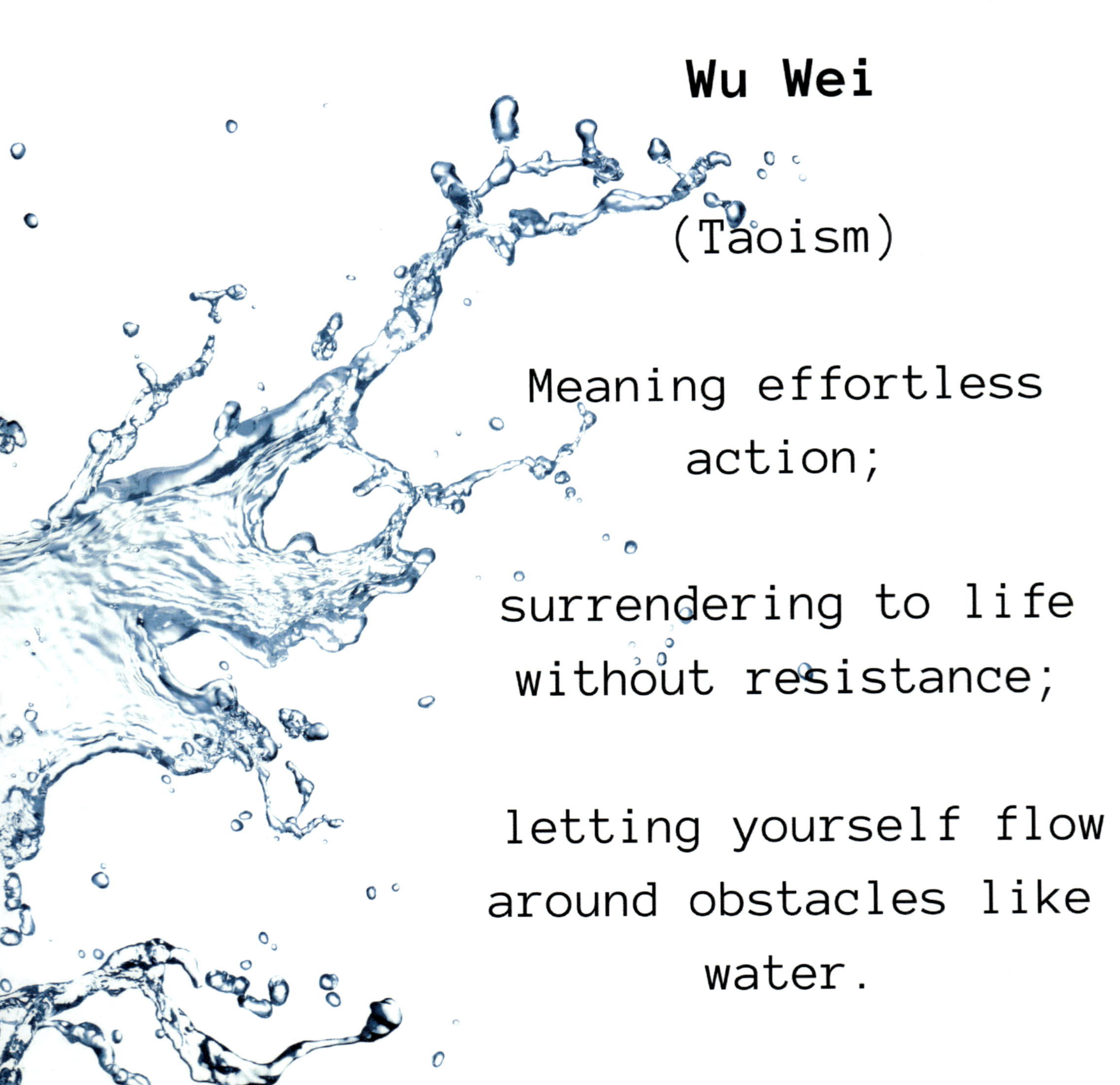

Wu Wei

(Taoism)

Meaning effortless action;

surrendering to life without resistance;

letting yourself flow around obstacles like water.

Xenodochial

(Greek)

means "friendly to strangers"

Do unto others as you would like done to yourself.

Yoga

The Yajur Veda, known as the "science of action," refines the ancient rishis' wisdom into rituals and transformative practices, notably yoga.

One of the major purposes of these actions is to support health and longevity.

Zenith

The highest point or
state that one can reach
in their spiritual
journey or enlightenment.

We are all on this
journey together.

Asé

The End

Made in the USA
Middletown, DE
23 May 2024

54711919R00033